Tsunamis

CHANA STIEFEL

Children's Press®
An Imprint of Scholastic Inc.
New York Toronto London Auckland Sydney
Mexico City New Delhi Hong Kong
Danbury, Connecticut

Content Consultant

K. Shafer Smith, Ph.D.
Associate Professor, Center for Atmosphere Ocean Science
Courant Institute of Mathematical Sciences
New York University
New York, NY

Library of Congress Cataloging-in-Publication Data

Stiefel, Chana, 1968-
  Tsunamis / by Chana Stiefel.
    p. cm. -- (A true book)
  Includes index.
      ISBN-13: 978-0-531-16885-1   (lib. bdg.)   978-0-531-21353-7   (pbk.)
      ISBN-10: 0-531-16885-9   (lib. bdg.)   0-531-21353-6   (pbk.)

1. Tsunamis--Juvenile literature. I. Title. II. Series.

GC221.5.S78 2009
551.46'37--dc22   2008014791

Produced by Weldon Owen Education Inc.

1 2 3 4 5 6 7 8 9 10 R 18 17 16 15 14 13 12 11 10 09

Find the Truth!

Everything you are about to read is true *except* for one of the sentences on this page.

Which one is **TRUE**?

T or F Elephants helped clean up after a major tsunami in 2004.

T or F Most tsunamis are caused by tornadoes.

Find the answers in this book.

3

Contents

THE **BIG** TRUTH!

Nature's Warning

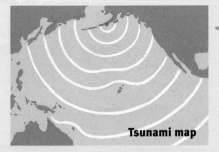

Tsunami map

A destructive, ocean-wide tsunami occurs about once every 15 years.

Coral

In Sumatra, Indonesia, many people live in villages near the ocean.

CHAPTER 1

Out of the Blue

December 26, 2004, started as a typical sunny day in Sumatra, Indonesia, an island in Southeast Asia. Ari Afrizal, a 21-year-old carpenter, was building a house on the beach. Suddenly, the ground started to shake. Without warning, a wave crashed into him. Then came a monster wave—a wall of water 30 feet (9 meters) high.

Indonesia is made up of more than 17,500 islands.

Fighting for Survival

The giant wave pushed Ari inland. He was tossed around like a rag in a huge washing machine. Ari tried to cling to tree branches. However, as the water pulled back, he was dragged out to sea.

Far from shore in the deep ocean, Ari first found a plank of wood to float on, then a leaky fishing boat. He survived on the milk and meat of coconuts he found floating in the storm debris. On his seventh day, Ari was lucky to find a large fishing raft with a hut on it. Finally, on the fifteenth day, Ari awoke to find a giant ship looming over him.

A sailor on a container ship took this photo of Ari Afrizal's raft just before Ari (below) was rescued.

Raft

Ari had just survived the most destructive tsunami in history. A tsunami is a series of huge waves triggered by a sudden movement of the ocean floor. This tsunami was caused by an earthquake beneath the Indian Ocean. In all, the tsunami claimed about 230,000 lives in 12 countries in Asia and Africa. Millions of people were left without homes, clothing, or food.

2004 Tsunami Map

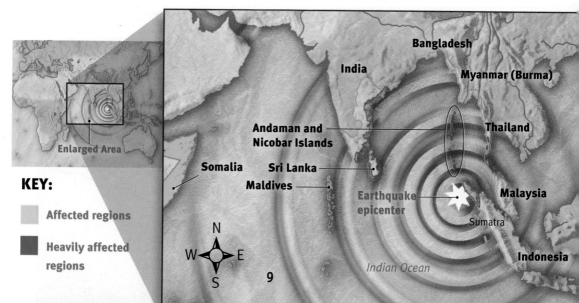

Bangladesh

India

Myanmar (Burma)

Andaman and
Nicobar Islands

Thailand

Enlarged Area

Somalia

Sri Lanka

Maldives

Earthquake
epicenter

Malaysia

Sumatra

KEY:

Affected regions

Heavily affected
regions

N
W E
S

Indian Ocean

Indonesia

9

First Hit

Banda Aceh (BAHN-duh AH-chay) is a city on the northern tip of Sumatra. It was one of the first cities to be hit by the tsunami waves. Banda Aceh was badly hit because it was close to the earthquake's **epicenter**. Some waves reached as high as 55 feet (17 meters). Within moments, coastal suburbs were flattened. Cars and fishing boats were tossed around like sticks. Thousands of people were swallowed by the sea. More than 120,000 people died.

This satellite photo shows Banda Aceh six months before the tsunami.

Banda Aceh is a changed city in this photo taken two days after the tsunami hit.

Tsunami waves charged across the Indian Ocean. About two hours after the earthquake, waves slammed into Sri Lanka, an island nation off the coast of India. The waves surged more than 1 mile (1.6 kilometers) inland. They flooded a train, killing more than 800 people. More than 35,000 Sri Lankans were killed.

Seven hours after the quake, tsunami waves crashed ashore in Africa. That's about 2,800 miles (4,500 kilometers) from the earthquake's epicenter.

Some people on the
Andaman Islands saw
the tsunami in time
to run for higher ground.

CHAPTER**2**

Tsunamis in Motion

Most tsunamis are caused by earthquakes under the ocean. Waves then speed in all directions, traveling far from the epicenter of the earthquake. A tsunami travels very fast. It can reach speeds of 600 miles (970 kilometers) per hour in the deep ocean. That's as fast as the speed of some airplanes.

The earthquake that caused the tsunami also triggered a volcanic eruption on the Andaman islands.

Shaky Earth

To understand how earthquakes cause tsunamis, think about the planet's rocky outer shell, or crust. The crust is broken up into massive slabs called **tectonic plates**. The plates fit together like pieces of a jigsaw puzzle. Tectonic plates are always in motion. They may slowly slide past, or push into, one another. Plate movement can result in a sudden release of energy. We call this an earthquake.

The boundary between two tectonic plates is called a fault.

The San Andreas fault in California lies between two plates that are sliding in opposite directions.

In deep water, a powerful tsunami may rise only a foot or two. Sailors on big ships could run over a tsunami without even realizing it.

Earthquakes give off waves of energy that move in all directions. Earthquakes under the sea send waves speeding through the water. In deep water, the waves spread out below the surface, so they are barely noticeable. However, the waves become more dangerous as they travel closer to land.

Ring of Disaster

If a tsunami is going to form, it's likely to start in the Pacific Ocean. About 85 percent of tsunamis strike there. Why? The Pacific is surrounded by faults, or boundaries between Earth's tectonic plates. Earthquakes, volcanoes, and landslides usually occur along faults. All these events can trigger tsunamis. The Pacific faults are so unstable that the area is called the Ring of Fire.

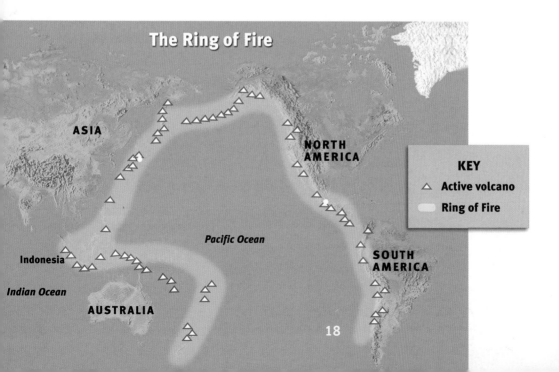

The Ring of Fire

ASIA

NORTH AMERICA

Pacific Ocean

Indonesia

Indian Ocean

AUSTRALIA

SOUTH AMERICA

KEY
△ Active volcano
▢ Ring of Fire

18

Volcanic Tsunamis

Sometimes, tsunamis can be triggered by volcanoes, falling **asteroids**, or **landslides**. Krakatau (krah-kuh-TAOW) is a volcanic island in Indonesia. Its eruption in 1883 was the most violent in recorded history. The island exploded, and two-thirds of it plunged into the sea. This triggered a tsunami. The waves were as high as 130 feet (40 meters). Tsunami waves killed about 35,000 people.

Krakatau before the 1883 eruption blew the mountain apart

Four months after the tsunami, life was still a struggle for survivors in Banda Aceh. Many were waiting for new homes to be built.

CHAPTER 3

Surviving the Waves

Millions of people got caught up in the 2004 tsunami. It didn't matter whether they were young or old, rich or poor. The world watched in shock and sorrow as the death toll increased in Asia and Africa. Yet survivors told tales of luck, quick thinking, bravery, and generosity.

← Two-thirds of the city Banda Aceh was destroyed by the 2004 tsunami.

Lucky Number 81

In Sri Lanka, a two-month-old baby was separated from his parents. He was thrown by the waves onto a heap of debris. Because no one knew his name, hospital workers nicknamed him Baby 81. He was the eighty-first patient they had seen that day. After two months and **genetic tests**, the baby was reunited with his parents. His real name was Abhilasha Jeyarajah.

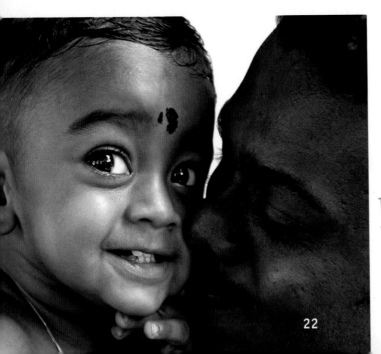

Abhilasha's parents struggled to prove he was their child. All their family records had been swept away.

Nine couples said that Baby 81 was their child!

Supermodel Survivor

A Czech fashion model, Petra Nemcova, was vacationing in Thailand when the tsunami struck. Waves swept her away. She survived by clinging onto a palm tree for nearly eight hours.

Having witnessed the tsunami and its impact, Nemcova started a charity to help children who have suffered from disasters. She has helped build schools, mobile medical units, and more.

The injured Petra Nemcova was reunited with her sister Olga in the Czech Republic.

Smart Student

Tilly Smith was on vacation in Thailand the day of the tsunami. The British schoolgirl was ten years old. She and her family were relaxing on the beach. Suddenly, Tilly noticed something strange. The sea looked frothy. Also, the water was receding from the shoreline, exposing the seafloor. Many people would have walked onto the uncovered sand to collect fish and seashells. Yet Tilly remembered something she had learned in school just two weeks earlier.

Tsunami Time Line

1883

The tsunami caused by the Krakatau eruption carries a warship 2 miles (3 kilometers) inland.

1949

The Pacific Tsunami Warning Center is set up after a tsunami strikes Hawai`i.

She recognized the unusual events as warning signs of a tsunami. Tilly began screaming for her family to run to higher ground. She and her parents alerted others to evacuate the beach. The family raced to the hotel's third floor just as the tsunami struck. They watched from their window. Waves engulfed everything in view. A quick-thinking schoolgirl had saved about a hundred lives.

Tilly Smith

1960

A huge earthquake near Chile creates a tsunami that travels all the way to Japan.

2004

The Red Cross feeds thousands of people affected by the Indian Ocean tsunami.

Vanishing Ocean

The sea looks much frothier than normal and is receding. There is a lot of seafloor left exposed.

Wall of Water

An enormous wave heads toward the beach. It's a tsunami!

Nature's Warning

Sometimes nature tells you that something unusual is happening. If more people had been aware of warning signs on the day of the Indian Ocean tsunami, more lives could have been saved. These illustrations show tsunami warning signs. Anyone who notices these should move to higher ground as quickly as possible.

Hidden Danger

Everything seems normal at the beach. Then you feel the earth move. It's an earthquake.

27

In Thailand, elephants were used to clean up rubble created by the killer tsunami.

CHAPTER 4

Cleaning Up

Once the waves receded from the 2004 tsunami, the scope of the devastation could be seen. The basic necessities of food, clean water, and shelter were unavailable for many people. Roads and millions of homes were in ruins. Electrical and telephone lines were down. Hospitals had been destroyed. The task ahead was enormous.

 Six elephants that had worked in movies helped to rescue tsunami survivors.

Helping Out

Televisions and newspapers all over the world showed images of the tsunami and the wreckage that followed it. Many people were motivated to help. Governments, international organizations, businesses, and individuals all helped in the recovery efforts.

Volunteers sorted through food donations for tsunami survivors in Sri Lanka.

Donations arrived in Banda Aceh, Indonesia, three days after the tsunami.

The worldwide community donated billions of dollars in aid to tsunami survivors.

Nations around the world sent food, water, clothing, medicine, and other supplies. Soldiers arrived to clear debris so that trucks could get through. Relief workers set up tents and other temporary homes. Doctors and nurses flew in from around the world. The quick international response helped to avert widespread hunger and disease.

The tsunami revealed a strong community spirit in the Maldives. People were happy to help their neighbors.

Rebuilding

Local people had a lot of cleaning up to do before they could start rebuilding. As they cleared away the debris, decisions were being made about what should be rebuilt and how it would be done. The idea was to "build back better." It was important that replacement buildings would be able to withstand floods, earthquakes, and severe weather.

The greatest challenge was to rebuild quickly and cheaply. Many new homes were made from bricks or concrete blocks. Block structures are affordable and sturdy. They also provide good **insulation**. Volunteers from around the world have helped with the long process of rebuilding.

In Sri Lanka, nearly a million people were left homeless by the disaster. Many aid agencies have helped build new homes.

TSUNAMI
EVACUATION
ROUTE

เส้นทางหนีคลื่นยักษ์

← 700 m.

Koh Lipe island, Thailand, is a popular holiday location. It now has tsunami evacuation route signs.

CHAPTER 5

Preventing Future Disasters

After the 2004 tsunami, people learned the importance of preparedness in reducing tsunami damage. They also learned the role the natural environment plays in tsunami protection. Many systems were put in place to protect against a repetition of the 2004 disaster.

Since 2005, tsunami warning signs have been put on beaches all over southern Thailand.

Sensing Tsunamis

The first step in keeping people safe is knowing when a tsunami forms. Scientists measure **seismic** activity on the ocean floor to spot tsunami triggers such as earthquakes. In addition, they use data from instruments called **tsunameters**. They also rely on knowledge of the shape of the ocean floor. Computers analyze this information to predict when a tsunami might strike, and how big it may become.

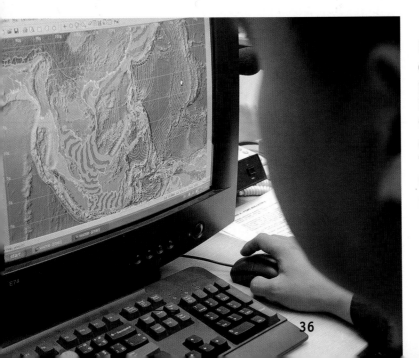

In 2006, 24 countries took part in the first international tsunami warning drill. Computers in Thailand tracked the fake tsunami's progress.

36

Tsunami Alert!

Deep in the Pacific Ocean lies modern technology that helps detect tsunamis when they first form. A tsunameter is a water pressure recorder that rests on the ocean floor. Water pressure varies according to wave height. The tsunameter sends the data it gathers to a nearby buoy. The buoy also monitors weather and water conditions on the surface. It sends all the data to a **satellite**. The satellite beams a radio signal to scientists at warning centers.

This buoy is a key part of a tsunami-predicting system.

Sending the Message

Detecting a tsunami is only the first step in saving lives. Governments need to alert people of the danger in time for them to evacuate. Because tsunamis are rare in the Indian Ocean, there were few warning systems in place there before the 2004 tsunami. Today, many beaches in Thailand are equipped with siren towers. Officials decide when the sirens will be used, based on information they receive from scientists.

Even a five-minute warning from this siren tower can allow sufficient time to escape an oncoming surge of water.

Run for Your Life

Many countries now have tsunami education programs to prepare people to act quickly. Schoolchildren and adults are taught to recognize the signs of a killer wave. They learn the best evacuation routes if there is enough advance warning. They also practice how to head for higher ground when waves are only minutes away.

Local children in Denpasar, Indonesia, practice responding to a tsunami warning.

Human Impact

Many scientists believe that people's changes to the environment can increase the damage caused by a tsunami. In many Asian countries, people have destroyed coral reefs to make room for shrimp farms, or to make the shoreline more accessible for ships. Reefs could help shield the shore from tsunamis by slowing down the waves.

In the Maldives, coral reefs reduced the impact of the 2004 tsunami. This may have helped save many lives.

Resort owners often removed sand dunes to give their guests a better view of the ocean.

Other human activities also contributed to the damage caused by the tsunami. Sand dunes on many beaches had been flattened. Many **mangrove forests** had been uprooted to make way for coastal resorts. Like coral reefs, sand dunes and mangrove forests help to protect the coast from tsunami waves.

Hope for the Future

The 2004 Indian Ocean tsunami served as a lesson to the global community. Countries have united to improve tsunami detection programs. Governments and citizens are becoming better prepared. People are working to protect coastal environments. They are hopeful that if they work together, the next tsunami will not be so disastrous. ★

In Indonesia, people have begun to plant mangrove trees to help shield the coast. The government has also put new environmental protection laws into place.

True Statistics

The decade in the 1900s with the most tsunamis: 1920–1929 (137 minor tsunamis, 12 major tsunamis)

Time it takes for a tsunami to cross the Pacific Ocean: Less than 24 hours

The U.S. state most at risk of a tsunami: Hawai`i (about 1 tsunami per year, on average)

Height of the 1958 Alaskan tsunami: About 1,700 feet (520 meters)

Likely trigger of the 1958 tsunami: A massive rockslide caused by an earthquake

Did you find the truth?

T Elephants helped clean up after a major tsunami in 2004.

F Most tsunamis are caused by tornadoes.

Resources

Books

Park, Louise. *Tsunamis*. North Mankato, MN: Smart Apple Media, 2008.

Rooney, Anne. *Tsunami!* (Nature's Fury). North Mankato, MN: Arcturus Publishing, 2006.

Scholastic Books. *Our Changing Planet: How Volcanoes, Earthquakes, Tsunamis, and Weather Shape Our Planet.* New York: Scholastic, Inc., 1996.

Spilsbury, Richard and Louise. *Tsunamis in Action* (Natural Disasters in Action). New York: Rosen Publishing Group, 2009.

Torres, John Albert. *Tsunami Disaster in Indonesia, 2004* (Natural Disasters). Hockessin, DEL: Mitchell Lane Publishers, 2006.

Woods, Michael and Mary B. *Tsunamis* (Disasters Up Close). Minneapolis, MN: Lerner Publications, 2007.

Organizations and Web Sites

West Coast and Alaska Tsunami Warning Center

http://wcatwc.arh.noaa.gov/book01.htm

Check out this *Tsunami Warning!* comic book, then create your own version.

National Data Buoy Center

www.ndbc.noaa.gov/dart.shtml

View real data from tsunameters (tsunami warning sensors) around the globe.

American Museum of Natural History

www.amnh.org/ology/earth/plates/index.html

Learn about the power of Earth's tectonic plates and how they affect our world.

Places to Visit

Pacific Tsunami Museum

130 Kamehameha Ave.
Hilo, HI 96720
(808) 935 0926
www.tsunami.org
Explore the science and history of tsunamis in the Pacific.

American Museum of Natural History

Central Park West at 79th St.
New York, NY 10024-5192
(212) 769 5100
www.amnh.org
Visit the Earthquake Monitoring Station to see where the seismic action is!

Important Words

asteroid (ASS-tuh-roid) – a small, rocky object that travels around the sun

epicenter – the part of Earth's surface directly above the place where an earthquake occurs

genetic tests – medical tests that analyze people's genetic material; genetic tests can show how people are related

insulation – a material that prevents heat from escaping or entering

landslide – the action of a large mass of earth and rock sliding down a slope at once

mangrove forest – a forest made up of mangrove trees; mangrove trees grow in shallow seawater

satellite – a natural or human-made object that circles a larger object in space

seismic (SIZE-mik) – relating to vibrations in the ground caused by earthquakes, explosions, or other events

tectonic plate – one of the large slabs of rock that make up Earth's outer crust

tsunameter (tsoo-NAHM-uh-tur) – an undersea device that detects and measures the waves of a tsunami

wavelength – the distance between the top of a wave and the top of the wave that follows it

Index

Page numbers in **bold** indicate illustrations

About the Author

Chana Stiefel has written several children's books about earthquakes, volcanoes, and other natural disasters. She is a former senior editor of Scholastic's *Science World* magazine. Ms. Stiefel holds a Master's degree in Journalism/Science and Environmental Reporting from New York University. She lives in Teaneck, New Jersey, with her husband and four children. Another True Book Earth Science title by Ms. Stiefel is *Thunderstorms*.

PHOTOGRAPHS: Anne Luo (p. 17); Digitalstock (p. 43); Getty Images (cover, p. 6; p. 12; p. 15; p. 19; p. 23; Tilly Smith, p. 25; p. 28; p. 31, pp. 38–39); Image Library: (background, pp. 26–27); International Federation of Red Cross and Red Crescent Societies (p. 33); iStockphoto.com (©George Clerk, p. 34; ©Imre Cikajlo, p. 41; © Le Do, coral, p. 5; ©Paul Cowan, Chilean flag, p. 25; T.MC, back cover); NOAA Center for Tsunami Research (p. 37); Tranz (Corbis, pp. 10–11; p. 20; p. 36; Reuters, p. 8; p. 22; p. 30; p. 40; p. 42); Yoshi Shimizu/ International Federation of Red Cross and Red Crescent Societies (volunteer serving food, p. 25; p. 32)

The publisher would like to thank Jorge Perez of the International Federation of Red Cross and Red Crescent Societies for supplying the photos on page 25, of a volunteer, and page 32.